MY FIRST 1000 WORDS

Wonder House

alphabet

Aa

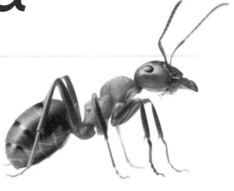

ant

Bb

boy

Cc

can

Dd

dinosaur

Ee

egg

Ff

fan

Gg

girl

Hh

hat

Ii

iron

Jj

jug

Kk

key

Ll

leaf

Mm

mouse

Nn

nest

Oo

ox

Pp

pen

Qq

quilt

Rr

rose

Ss

soap

Tt

tap

Uu

urn

Vv

vase

Ww

wheel

Xx

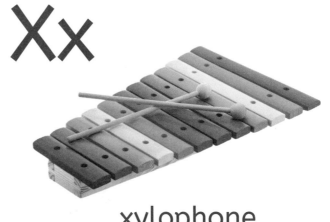

xylophone

Yy

yarn

Zz

zip

numbers

1 one

2 two

3 three

4 four

5 five

6 six

7 seven

8 eight

9 nine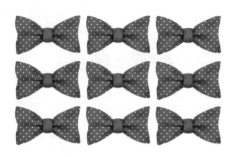

10 ten

11
eleven

12
twelve

13
thirteen

14
fourteen

15
fifteen

16
sixteen

17
seventeen

18
eighteen

19
nineteen

20
twenty

colors

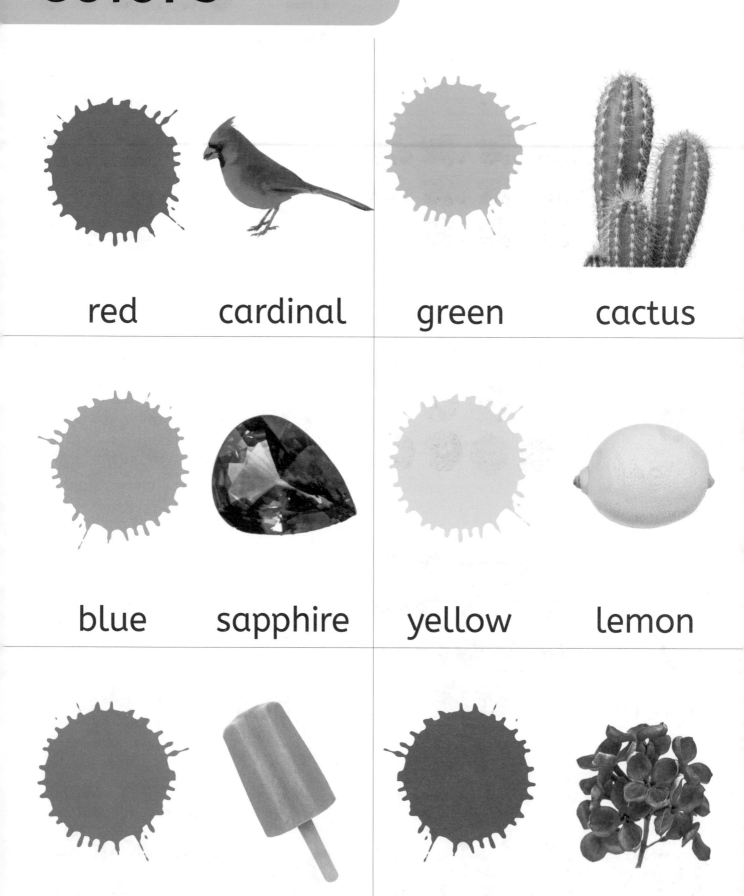

red   cardinal   green   cactus

blue   sapphire   yellow   lemon

orange   ice candy   violet   lilac

pink   cotton candy

gray   dustbin

black   coal

brown   chocolate

white   igloo

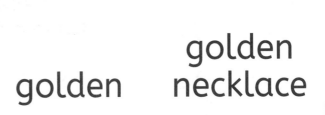

golden   golden necklace

shapes

circle

wheel

button

square

cracker

chessboard

rectangle

envelope

playing card

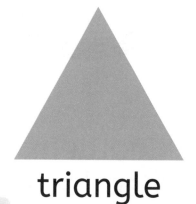

triangle

sandwich

traffic sign

cone

ice cream cone

traffic cone

oval

mirror

gemstone

diamond

kite

earring

heart

balloon

crescent

moon

star

starfish

11

opposites

slow   fast

few   many

hot   cold

soft   hard

front   back

inside   outside

| empty | full | dirty | clean |

| big | small | heavy | light |

| open | closed | happy | sad |

 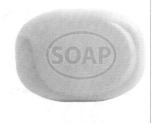  

| rough | smooth | old | new |

fruits

apple   orange   watermelon   coconut

banana   pineapple   peach   mango

cantaloupe   papaya   cherry   pear

grape   pomegranate   kiwi   avocado

date strawberry blueberry fig

guava grapefruit apricot

dragon fruit custard apple raspberry

blackberry starfruit plum

cranberry litchi gooseberry

vegetables

cauliflower   cabbage   green bell pepper   carrot

pumpkin   zucchini   spinach   corn

okra   lettuce   leek   radish

onion   turnip   potato   sweetpotato

red bell pepper   **french bean**   **broccoli**   **kale**

beetroot   **green pea**   **eggplant**   **spring onion**

yam   **artichoke**   **bottle gourd**   **ginger**

garlic   **cucumber**   **asparagus**   **celery**

food

milk

sushi

salad

tofu

taco

cornflakes

soup

ice cream

juice

waffle

fish

chicken

pie

shrimp

rice

cereal

| mushroom | cheese | trail mix | pasta |

| yogurt | pancake | macaroni | pizza |

| cookie | muffin | butter | bread |

| hummus | honey | oatmeal | popcorn |

transport

bicycle

tandem

skateboard

unicycle

scooter

motorcycle

car

taxi

van

go-cart

snowmobile

golf cart

bus   lorry   garbage truck

  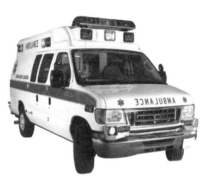

fire engine   truck   ambulance

tractor   tow truck   food wagon

digger   oil tanker   caravan

train   cable car   tram

airplane   hot-air balloon   helicopter

blimp   rocket   space shuttle

parachute   jet   seaplane

fishing boat   **kayak**   **yacht**

ferry   **jet ski**   **raft**

cargo ship   **sailboat**   **boat**

ship   **submarine**   **hovercraft**

people at work

baker   chef   detective   lawyer   doctor

police
officer

teacher

farmer

mechanic

soldier

musician   firefighter   carpenter   florist

astronaut   scientist   architect   delivery person

photographer   pilot   hairdresser   artist

birds

parrot

peacock

owl

swan

woodpecker

kingfisher

crow

sparrow

pigeon

penguin

vulture eagle flamingo

zebra finch ostrich crane

puffin hummingbird mynah

robin toucan hornbill

pets & farm animals

dog   cat   sheep   rabbit

goat   cow   bull

horse   camel   llama

yak

donkey

hen

buffalo

alpaca

emu

rooster

ferret

guinea pig

hamster

duck

goose

turkey

wild animals

tiger

lion

giraffe

zebra

wolf

kangaroo

deer

fox

bear

polar bear

rhinoceros

cheetah

hippopotamus   panda   elephant

monkey   hyena   boar

gorilla   porcupine   chameleon

crocodile   koala   lemur

baby animals

puppy   kitten   cow calf   horse foal

lion cub   tiger cub   chick   duckling

deer
fawn

donkey
foal

giraffe
calf

zebra
foal

penguin chick   lamb   bear cub

kit   kid   owlet

parrot chick   elephant calf   rhinoceros calf

baby tortoise   polar bear cub   swan cygnet

sea animals

clownfish

angelfish

balloonfish

pilot whale

dolphin

jellyfish

sea turtle

shark

seahorse

eel

swordfish

clam

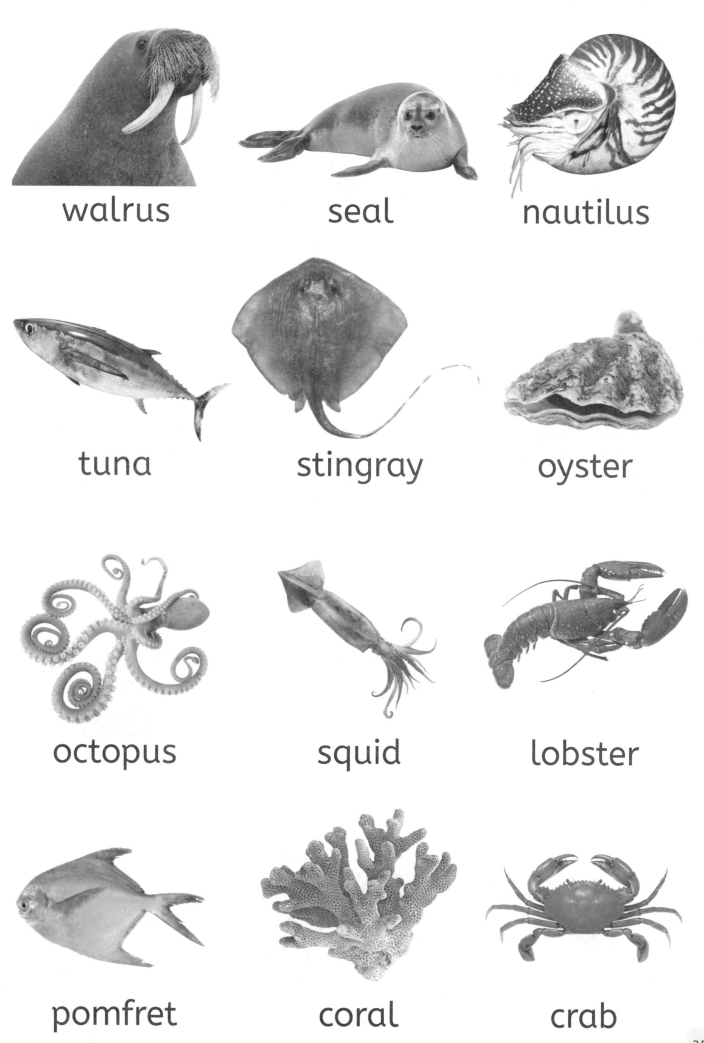

walrus

seal

nautilus

tuna

stingray

oyster

octopus

squid

lobster

pomfret

coral

crab

insects

ant

butterfly

mosquito

bee

moth

grasshopper

stick insect

dragonfly

beetle

scorpion

spider

cockroach

my body

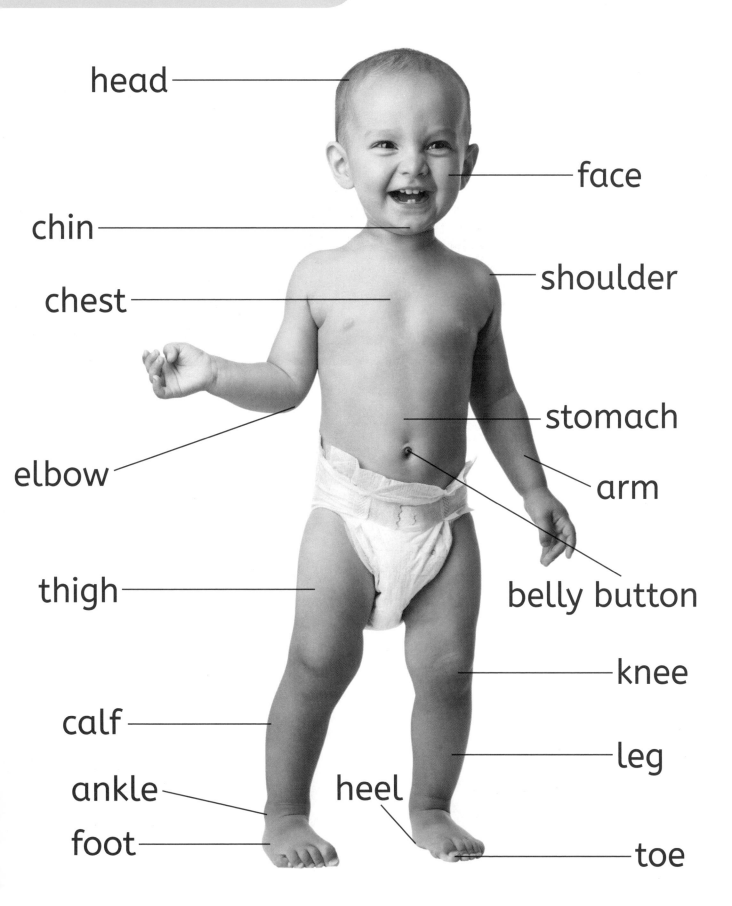

head

face

chin

shoulder

chest

stomach

elbow

arm

thigh

belly button

knee

calf

leg

ankle

heel

foot

toe

my face

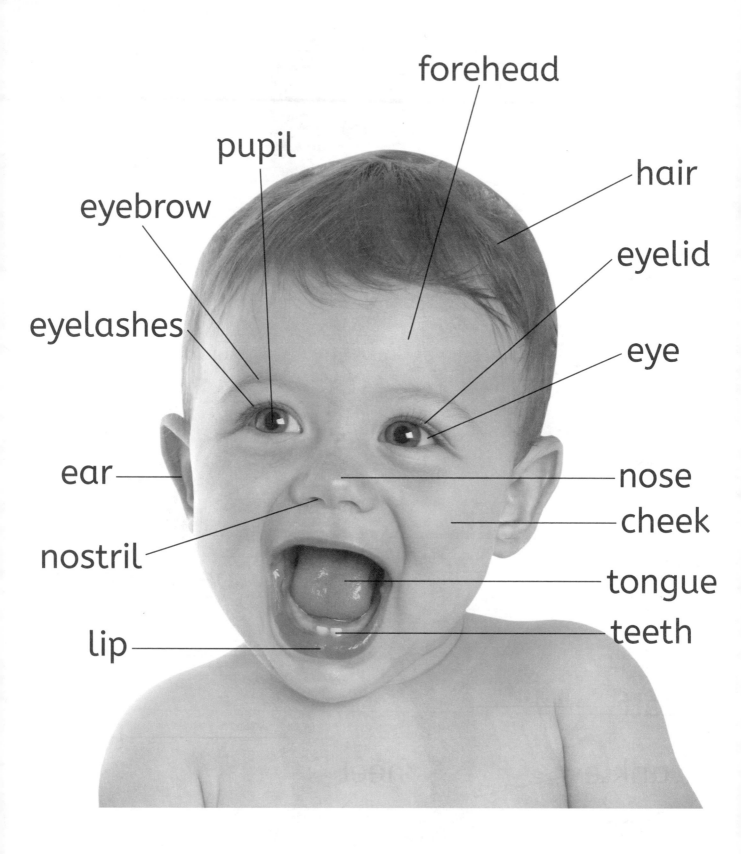

forehead

pupil

eyebrow

hair

eyelid

eyelashes

eye

ear

nose

cheek

nostril

lip

tongue

teeth

my hands

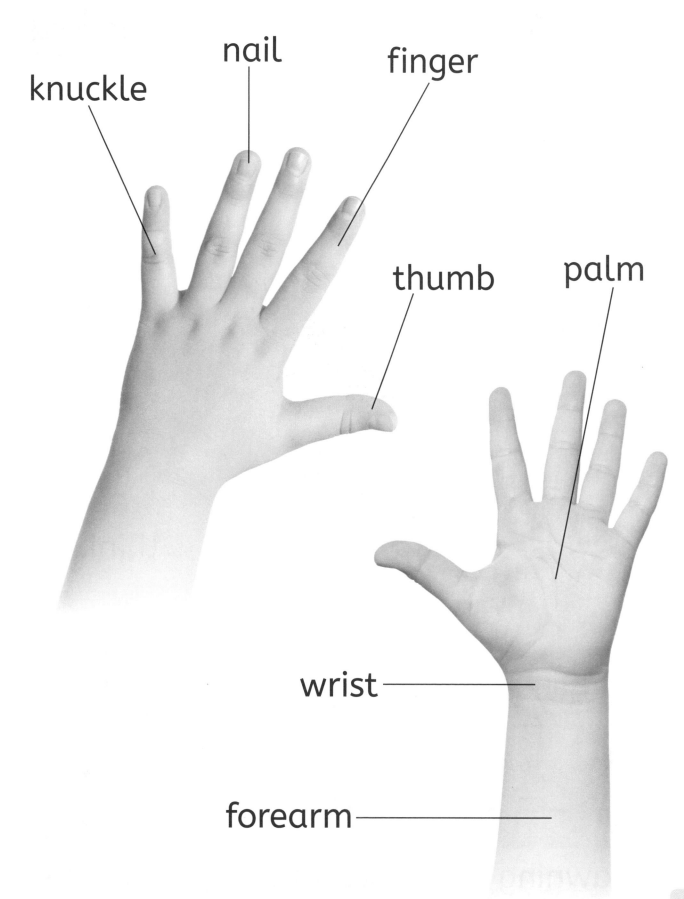

knuckle

nail

finger

thumb

palm

wrist

forearm

baby faces

laughing

crying

smiling

surprised

excited

thinking

yawning

worried

scared

my senses

touch

hear

sight

smell

taste

toys

 toy car

 rattle

 dinosaur

 bath toy

 chinese checkers

 top

 dollhouse

 rubik's cube

 robot

 train set

 rocking horse

 skipping rope

tricycle

blocks

kitchen set

finger puppet

mask

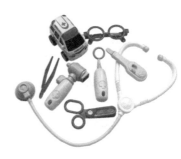
toy phone

soft toy

ring stacker

doctor set

jigsaw puzzle

musical keyboard

marble

toy tunnel

push-along toy

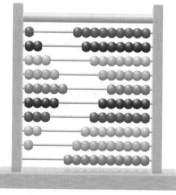

bowling set

labyrinth

tumbler

abacus

ring toss

pinwheel

remote control car

magic board

hula hoop

toy car

building blocks

tic-tac-toe

play mat

doll

shape sorter

frisbee

yo-yo

space hopper ball

microphone

toy storage box

baby objects

bib

sipper

high chair

milk bottle

blanket

crib

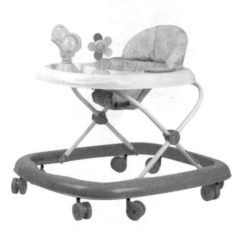
walker

stroller

ball

shoes

potty seat

bath tub

baby rocker

car seat

comb

romper

spoon

bowl

baby pillow

mosquito net

bag

baby oil

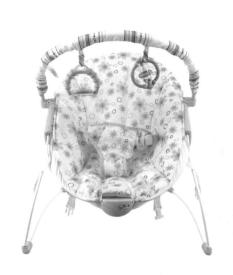

baby bouncer

teether

baby
powder

cot mobile

toothbrush

booties

 dresser

 mitten

 bassinet

 baby carrier

 crayons

 baby food

 mattress

 photo frame

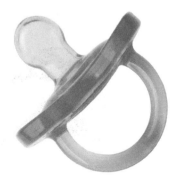 pacifier

living room

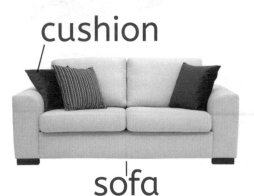
cushion

sofa

armchair

center table

carpet

curtain

television

wall clock

telephone

fireplace

hanging light

air
conditioner

vase

duvet

pillow

bed

wardrobe

dressing table

bean bag

radio

doormat

alarm clock

window

table lamp

fan

ironing board

chest of drawers

bathroom

 soap dish

 cabinet

 mouth freshener

 shower

 laundry hamper

 toilet pot

 washbasin

 loofah

 mug

 toilet paper

 mirror

 bath brush

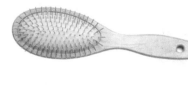 hairbrush

toothpaste

shampoo

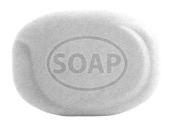

soap

towel

tissue paper

blinds

exhaust fan

hair oil

sponge

washing machine

washing powder

cotton swab

hair dryer

kitchen

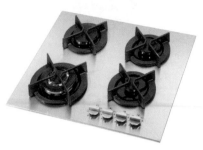

gas stove

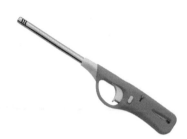

gas lighter

chimney

chopping board

spatula

plate

rolling pin

pressure cooker

cutlery

tray

jar

glass

sink

54

dishwasher

refrigerator

microwave oven

cup

saucer

saucepan

apron

tea towel

frying pan

grill

coffee maker

whisk

blender

kettle

toaster

garden

grass

hedge

leaves

honeycomb

nest

tree

sticks

caterpillar

earthworm

garden hose

watering can

greenhouse   birdhouse   garden fork   rake

ladybug   wasp   lawnmower   waste bin

seeds   spade   wheelbarrow   bricks

kennel   sprinkle   trowel   flowerpot

school

book

chalk

blackboard

students

marker

whiteboard

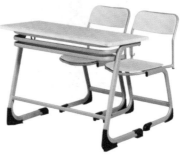
desk

lamp

clay

pen
corrector

drawing

easel

notebook

pencil

calculator

eraser

ruler   duster   felt tip pen   watercolor

brush   softboard   globe   badge

glue   tack   computer   waste bin

aquarium   calendar   paper

park

bench

merry-go-round

slide

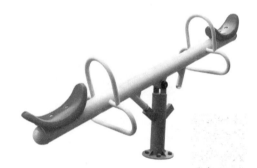
see-saw

swing

sandpit

picnic basket

children

fountain

 flower bed

 roller skates

 lamp post

 pushchair

 gate

 fence

 monkey bars

 path

 tree

 playhouse

 jungle gym

 statue

sports

cycling

cricket

hockey

baseball

basketball

table tennis

chess

archery

gymnastics

judo

football

rugby

tennis

badminton

ice skating

golf

camping

backpack

first aid kit

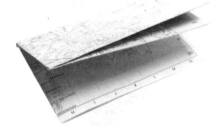

map

sleeping bag

tent

water bottle

battery

torch

lantern

compass

thermos

hiking boots

camping stove

lighter

camera

binoculars

video camera

 hat

 sunglasses

sandcastle

 umbrella

 swimming ring

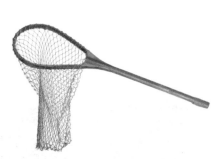 fishing net

flag

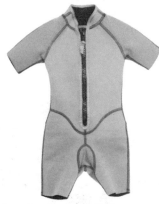 diving suit

diving mask

 flippers

 sunscreen

 swimsuit

island

surfboard

beach toy

lighthouse

rope

seaweed

shell

pebbles

seagull

mat

clothes

shawl

shorts

gloves

scarf

jacket

sweatshirt

night dress

pyjamas

t-shirt

shirt

skirt

socks

 sweater

 cardigan

  gown

 trousers

 raincoat

 overalls

 woolen cap

 jeans

 suit

blazer

 tie

 coat

party

party glasses

party mask

cold drink

paper chain

party popper

popsicle

party hat

teddy bear

party dress

gifts

lightbulb

slush

donuts

chocolate
pudding

tablecloth

ribbon

tiara

straw

candle

circus

clown

hoop

ringmaster

circus tent

juggling

clown's cap

clown's bow

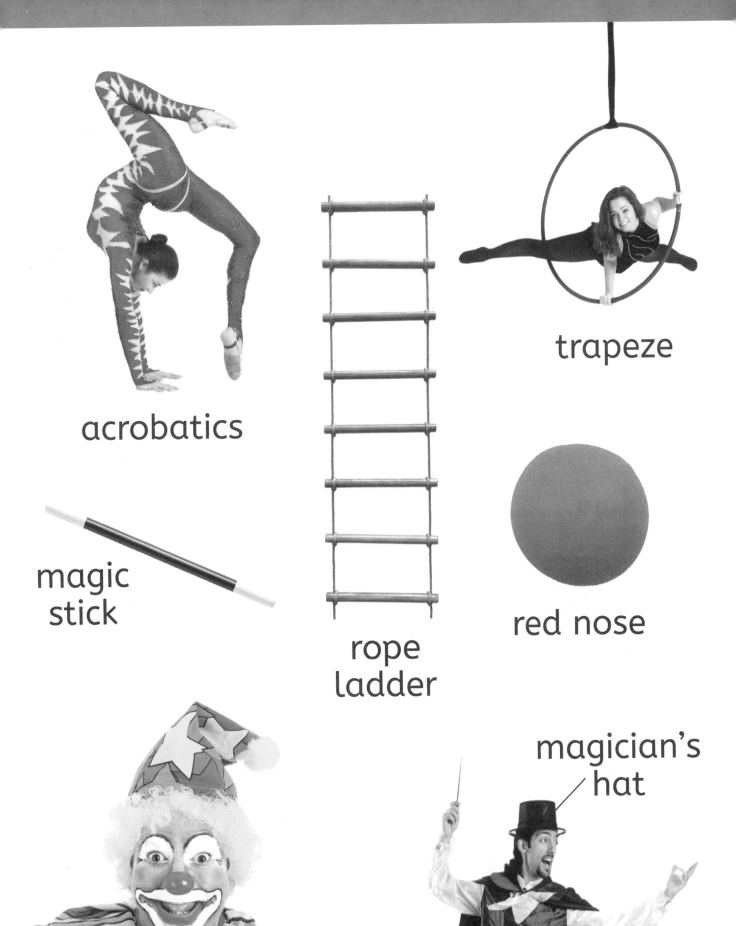

acrobatics

trapeze

magic stick

rope ladder

red nose

face paint

magician's hat

magician

words in a story

fairy

queen

crown

king

princess prince

castle

warrior

sword

shield

bow

arrow

unicorn   knight   pirate   treasure

broomstick

wizard   witch   vampire

monster   dragon   mermaid   wand

action words

laugh

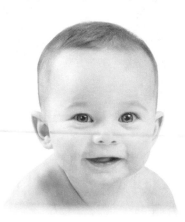

smile

eat

drink

read

play

talk

write

angry

cry

crawl

climb

walk

catch

pick

throw

sleep

bend

wash

pull

dance

paint

listen

think

hide   kneel   cut

sweep   sing

run   kick   carry

flowers

sunflower

marigold

iris

lotus

tulip

carnation

lily

canna

jasmine

pansy

rose

daisy

daffodil   hyacinth   periwinkle

zinnia   dahlia   poppy

petunia   orchid   morning glory

hibiscus   bougainvillea   buttercup

musical instruments

xylophone

violin

guitar

lute

ukulele

flute

clarinet

maraca

piano

synthesizer

cymbal

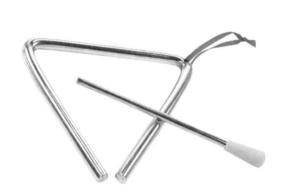

triangle

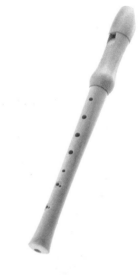

recorder

mandolin

bongo drum

drum

gong

tabla

harp

sitar

harmonium

tambourine

dhol

harmonica

bagpipes

accordion

tuba

banjo

trumpet

saxophone

trombone

french horn

hospital

nurse

patient

stethoscope

doctor

sticking
plaster

bandage

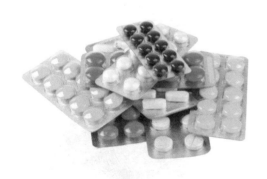

medicine

syrup

thermometer

walking
stick

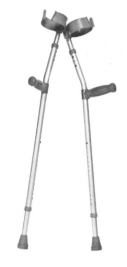
crutches

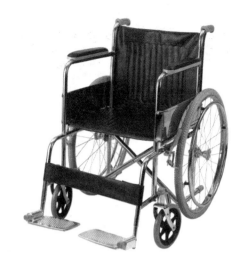
wheelchair

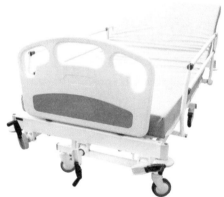
hospital
bed

medical
gloves

surgical
mask

plaster

stretcher

medical
tray

accessories

ring

key chain

earring

hairband

bracelet

hair clips

clutch

purse

belt

wrist watch

bowtie

words list

a

abacus, 44
accessories, 88
accordion, 85
acrobatics, 73
action words, 76
air conditioner, 50
airplane, 22
alarm clock, 51
alpaca, 29
alphabet, 2
ambulance, 21
angelfish, 34
angry, 77
ankle, 37
ant, 2,36
apple, 14
apricot, 15
apron, 55
aquarium, 59
archery, 62
architect, 25
armchair, 50
arm, 37
arrow, 74
artichoke, 17
artist, 25
asparagus, 17
astronaut, 25
avocado, 14

b

baby animals, 32
baby bouncer, 48
baby carrier, 49
baby faces, 40
baby food, 49

baby objects, 46
baby oil, 48
baby pillow, 47
baby powder, 48
baby rocker, 47
baby tortoise, 33
back, 12
backpack, 64
badge, 59
badminton, 63
bagpipes, 85
bag, 48
baker, 24
boy, 2
ball,46
balloon, 11
balloonfish, 34
banana, 14
bandage, 86
banjo, 85
baseball, 62
basketball, 62
bassinet, 49
bath brush, 52
bath toy, 42
bathroom, 52
bathtub, 47
battery, 64
beanbag, 51
bear, 30
bear cub, 33
beach toy, 67
bed, 51
bedroom, 51
bee, 36
beetle, 36
beetroot, 17
belly button, 37

belt, 89
bench, 60
bend, 78
bib, 46
bicycle, 20
big, 13
binoculars, 65
birdhouse, 57
birds, 26
black, 9
blackberry, 15
blackboard, 58
blanket, 46
blazer, 69
blender, 55
blimp, 22
blinds, 53
blocks, 43
blue, 8
blueberry, 15
boar, 31
boat, 23
book, 58
booties, 48
bongo drum, 83
bottle gourd, 17
boungainvillea, 81
bow, 74
bowl, 47
bowling set, 44
bowtie, 89
box, 5
bracelet, 88
bread, 19
bricks, 57
broccoli, 17
broomstick, 75
brown, 9

brush, 59
buffalo, 29
building blocks, 45
bull, 28
bus, 21
bush, 60
butter, 19
button, 10
buttercup, 81
butterfly, 36

c

cabbage, 16
cabinet, 52
cable car, 22
cactus, 8
calender, 59
calculator, 58
calf, 37
camel, 28
camera, 65
camping, 64
camping stove, 65
can, 2
candle, 71
canna, 80
cantaloupe, 14
car, 20
caravan, 21
cargo ship, 23
car seat, 47
cardigan, 69
cardinal, 8
carnation, 80
carpenter, 25
carpet, 50
carrot, 16

p

pacifier, 49
paddle, 23
paint, 78
palm, 39
pancake, 19
pansy, 80
panda, 31
papaya, 14
paper chain, 70
paper, 59
park, 60
parrot, 26
parrot chick, 33
party, 70
party dress, 70
party hat,70
party glasses, 70
party mask, 70
party popper, 70
parachute, 22
pasta, 19
path, 61
patient, 86
peach, 14
peacock, 26
pear, 14
pebbles, 67
pen corrector, 58
pen, 4
pencil, 58
penguin, 26
penguin chick, 33
people at work, 24
periwinkle, 81
pet animals, 28
petunia, 81
photo frame, 49
photographer, 25
piano, 83
pick, 77

picnic basket, 60
pie, 18
pigeon, 26
pillow, 51
pilot, 25
pineapple, 14
pink, 9
pinwheel, 44
pirate, 75
pizza, 19
plaster, 87
plate, 54
play mat, 45
playhouse, 61
plum, 15
polar bear, 30
polar bear cub, 33
police officer, 24
pomegranate, 14
pomfret, 35
poppy, 81
popsicle, 70
porcupine, 31
potato, 16
popcorn ,19
potty seat, 47
pressure cooker, 54
prince, 74
princess, 74
pull, 78
puffin, 27
pumpkin, 16
pupil, 38
puppy, 32
purse, 89
pushchair, 61
push along toy, 44
pyjamas, 68

q

quilt, 4
queen, 74

r

rabbit, 28
radio, 51
radish, 16
raft, 23
rake, 57
raincoat, 69
raspberries, 15
rattle, 42
read, 76
rectangle, 10
recorder, 83
red, 8
red bell pepper, 17
red nose, 73
remote control car, 44
refrigerator, 55
rhinoceros, 30
rhinoceros calf, 33
ribbon, 71
rice, 18
ring stacker, 43
ring, 88
ring toss, 44
ringmaster, 72
robin, 27
robot, 42
rocket, 22
rocking horse, 42
roller skates, 61
rolling pin, 54
romper, 47
rooster, 29
rope ladder, 73
rope, 67
rose, 4, 80
rough, 13

rubik's cube, 42
rugby, 63
ruler, 59
run, 79

s

sad, 13
sailboat, 23
salad, 18
sandcastle, 66
sandpit, 60
sandwich, 10
sapphire, 8
saucepan, 55
saucer, 55
saxophone, 85
scarf, 68
scared, 40
school, 58
scientist, 25
scooter, 20
scorpion, 36
sea animals, 34
seaplane, 22
sea turtle, 34
seagull, 67
seahorse, 34
seal, 35
seaside, 66
seaweed, 67
seeds, 57
see-saw, 60
seven, 6
seventeen, 7
shampoo, 53
shapes, 10
shape sorter, 45
shark, 34
shawl, 68
sheep, 28
shell, 67
shield, 74